The Pets at Home guide to

Rabbits

Expert advice on caring for your pet

Carrots and other vegetables are better for your rabbit's health than lots of sweetened snacks, but introduce fresh foods gradually if your pet is not used to them .

Published by Interpet Publishing,
Vincent Lane, Dorking,
Surrey RH4 3YX, England.

Hardback ISBN 13: 978-1-84286-129-5
Hardback ISBN 10: 1-84286-129-8

Paperback ISBN 13: 978-1-84286-124-0
Paperback ISBN 10: 1-84286-124-7

Publishing credits
Editor: Anne McDowall
Consultant: Emma Magnus
Designed and prepress: Philip Clucas MSI
Production management: Consortium, Poslingford, Suffolk
Print production: Sino Publishing House L
Hong Kong
Printed and bound in China

CONTENTS

Introducing Rabbits

Understanding where rabbits come from and how they live

Rabbits have been popular with children and adults alike for decades. Despite all coming from a single wild species (Oryctolagus cuniculus)*, the many different breeds vary hugely in size and suitability as pets (see chapter 2, pages 10–23), but a medium-sized rabbit can make a good companion whether kept in the house or in a hutch outside.*

However, although a rabbit can become relatively friendly and tame, it will not be content to sit still on a child's lap for long periods of time and its strong hind legs can kick hard. For this reason, a rabbit is not the ideal choice for a young child less than about seven years old, and even an older child may be unable to handle a large breed properly. (A guinea pig or rat would make a better pet for a young child.)

abbits as pets

Rabbits are believed to have a history of more than 4000 years and they have been kept in domestication since Roman times. Originally from the Mediterranean area, they have since been introduced by man across Europe, into the UK and to Australia, New Zealand and the USA.

For many hundreds of years, they were bred solely for their fur and their meat and were kept in large enclosures known as warrens, but as more people moved from the countryside into towns, they began to house rabbits in hutches to provide themselves with meat. People began keeping rabbits simply as pets only in the 19th century.

tip

Give it time

Although a rabbit is not difficult to look after, you will need to give it attention if you want it to develop into a tame pet.

Rabbits are inquisitive: a fence like this is fine for playtimes, but it won't prevent escapes.

WHY KEEP A RABBIT?

Rabbits are among the most popular small pets – and with good reason. They are:

- **responsive and entertaining** – provided that you choose a suitable breed and are prepared to spend time with it.
- **resilient and adaptable** – a rabbit will live much longer (generally five years or more) than other smaller pets, such as hamsters or gerbils.
- **suitable as indoor or outdoor pets** – see chapter 3 for information on housing.
- **relatively long-lived** – your rabbit may be with you for eight to ten years.

Understanding Your Rabbit – how it lives

Pet rabbits are descended from wild animals and have retained many of the physical traits and behaviour patterns of their wild ancestors and cousins that were developed to enable them to survive as prey animals. Gaining an insight into how rabbits live in the wild will help you to better understand, and thus care for, your pet rabbit.

Life in the wild

Wild rabbits live in extensive networks of burrows in the ground that are known as warrens. These warrens are used by generations of rabbits and well-developed ones will have many entrances and exits, areas for sleeping and even nursery runs for litters.

Rabbits are vegetarians, feeding on grass and vegetables and, when greens are scarce, on bark. They gain maximum nutritional benefit from their food by eating the first set of droppings that they produce.

Food should not be in short supply for your pet rabbit, but it will still enjoy nibbling on the bark of an apple twig. The grey-brown coloration of this pet rabbit is the same as that of its wild cousins.

Lop-eared breeds do not have such good hearing as other breeds, for whom this is the most important sense.

he rabbit's senses

Like other small prey animals, a rabbit has very good long sight and all-round vision. Its eyes are situated towards the top of its head and each eye has a 190° field of vision, which means that the rabbit can see if it is about to be attacked. Its near-distance vision is very poor, however, which means that it will be easily startled.

Until your rabbit has become accustomed to your smell (which it will use, rather than sight, to identify you), keep your hands above its head and away from its nose. Your rabbit may nip you if it is scared, you move suddenly or if it mistakes your fingers for food.

Rabbits have a much better sense of smell than humans. Unfamiliar smells will be alarming to your rabbit so make sure that you always wash your hands before, as well as after, touching your pet (but avoid using strong-smelling soap or creams on your hands). A rabbit will mark its territory – with its urine, droppings and using scent glands under its chin – to make a place feel like home and deter any potential intruders.

Hearing *This is the most highly developed sense. The ears move independently to pick up as much sound as possible.*

Sight *Long-distance vision is excellent, but your rabbit may not be able to see you close-up.*

mell *A rabbit uses its sense of smell o find food, detect danger and learn about other individuals.*

Touch *The rabbit's sensitive upper lip tells it whether an item is edible or not.*

tip

Approach a new rabbit slowly

Your hand suddenly appearing in front of its face will be very unsettling to your rabbit, particularly if it hasn't had time to get used to your smell.

Rabbit intelligence

Rabbits are not known for their intelligence, but while they are certainly less intelligent than a dog or a cat, they rank above most other small pets, such as guinea pigs, hamsters or gerbils. Your rabbit can certainly learn to respond to you calling its name and can be house-trained and taught to walk on a lead. Some owners have even taught their rabbits to jump small fences and to be clean in the house!

Rabbit behaviour

Unlike many other animals – cats and dogs, for example – rabbits don't communicate with sounds. Their vocal noises are generally limited to grunts (angry, a warning to back off or be bitten) and tooth-grinding (usually a sign of contentment). They will scream only in situations of extreme terror or pain.

Most rabbits can be trained to toilet in a litter tray filled with wood shavings or a non-clumping cat litter.

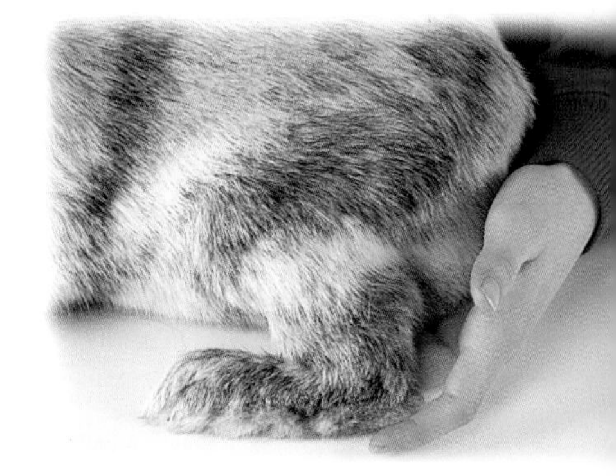

A rabbit's hind legs are much larger and stronger than its forelegs and can pack a powerful punch. They can also be used to make quite a noise when the rabbit stamps on the ground.

RABBIT BODY LANGUAGE

What your rabbit does	What it means
Stamps loudly on the ground	A warning of impending danger. Your rabbit may also stamp to summon you.
Nips you	Rabbits nip out of fear or aggression but if your rabbit nips you it may just mean it has had enough attention.
Sprays urine over its hutch	Male rabbits (bucks), in particular, will mark their territory by spraying urine. Females (does) may also mark during the spring.
Rubs its chin against objects or against you	Rabbits have glands under their chins that secrete a scent. As with spraying urine, your rabbit will do this to mark its territory.
Lashes out with its forelegs	This aggressive behaviour is particularly noticeable in does that are nursing young. It means 'Get out of my hutch!'
Goes round and round in circles making a low purring noise	When a buck does this, he is looking for a doe to mate.
Rolls over on its back	Provided your rabbit is still breathing, this is no cause for alarm! Your rabbit is just feeling thoroughly contented.
Running around with tufts of hay or other bedding in its mouth	A doe will do this as she prepares a nest. Your rabbit may be pregnant or just feeling broody.

tip

Check the teeth of an aggressive rabbit

If your previously placid rabbit becomes aggressive, ask your vet to check its teeth. Overgrown teeth or spurs on the side of teeth can cause a rabbit discomfort, which may make it behave aggressively.

Rabbits are naturally inquisitive animals and you will soon learn to recognize curiosity and your pet's emotions in its body language and behaviour.

Rabbit Breeds

Choosing the right rabbit for your level of experience

There are more than 60 known breeds of rabbit, all of which are descended from the wild one. Many of these breeds come in a variety of colours, coat types and, often, sizes, from giant ones larger than a cat to miniature ones that will fit in your hand. Fur types include Rexes, which have short plush coats, Satins, with smooth, very shiny coats, and longhairs, such as the fluffy Cashmere Lop and profusely coated Angora.

tip

Check temperament

A few rabbits, particularly some of the smaller varieties, can be aggressive if they are nervous. To assess the temperament of a young rabbit you are thinking of buying, try to get the opportunity to handle it.

Medium-sized breeds are best as pets for children. They tend to be less nervous than small breeds and are lighter than large ones.

ırge or small?

The largest rabbit breeds include the French Lop (see page 18) and Flemish Giant, ɔoth of which are about three times the size of a wild rabbit, weighing around 11.5kg (25lb). Although such large animals will be difficult for children to handle, larger breeds are generally calmer than the miniature ones and they make gentle pets. Their main disadvantages are their need for larger accommodation and their shorter lifespan, often as little as four or five years.

Miniature breeds, such as the Netherland Dwarf and Polish (see page 16), are undoubtedly cute, but they are not cuddly. As they are small, they can tend to be more nervous and highly strung than their larger counterparts and are more likely to nip. They are therefore not recommended as children's pets. However, they include the longest-lived breeds, averaging 10–12 years, and many smaller rabbits will respond to gentle handling and develop into confident little animals.

Netherland Dwarfs are among the smallest of all pet rabbits, weighing no more than 0.9kg (2lb).

Grouping of breeds

In the UK, rabbit breeds are grouped into Fancy, Fur and Rex breeds and this is the way we have organized the breeds featured in this chapter. In the USA and some other countries, rabbits are divided into groups according to their weight. Lop-eared rabbits, or Lops, are actually classified under Fancy breeds, but as there are several different Lop breeds, most of which are very popular, we have presented these separately.

Sussex (see page 17)

CROSSBREED RABBITS

Many rabbits you see for sale will be crossbreeds, and rabbits bred from mixed parentage can make perfectly good pets. The main disadvantage with buying a crossbreed rabbit is that, if you buy a youngster, you won't know what size it will end up. Neither will you know what sort of temperament it is likely to have. With a purebred rabbit, you can expect it to resemble its parents.

Rabbit Colours and Markings

Most of the many different breeds of rabbits come in a huge variety of colours. Some of the colour names are self-explanatory, others are less so. The following are some of the more common rabbit colours and markings or patterns that you may come across, many of which may also be found on different coat types.

Agouti The hairs on an agouti are two toned in appearance with more than one colour on each strand. The normal agouti is the colour of the wild rabbit – a grey-brown colour (see picture 3 opposite) – but other colours may also be a version of the agouti.

Black Ideally the colour should be very dense. The underfur of a black rabbit is usually a blue-grey colour.

Blue This colour should be an even blue-grey.

Broken Marked Like the butterfly (see below) but with varied markings on a white background.

Butterfly Rabbits with this pattern are white and have a butterfly-shaped coloured marking on the nose. They also have coloured ears and patches around the eyes, a large coloured patch on the back and variable amounts of spotting.

Chinchilla Like the animal of that name, chinchilla rabbits appear almost silver (see Fur Breeds, pages 20–21). This is a version of the agouti in which all the brown pigmentation is replaced with white. The undercolour is dark blue, the middle colour is white and each hair is tipped with black.

Chocolate This should be an even brow colour.

Fawn (or Yellow) The topcoat is a brig fawn shade, the underfur almost white. Fawn-coloured rabbits have a white belly

1

1: Blue (left) and Black Otter (right) Netherland Dwarfs. 2: Opal Netherland Dwarf. 3: Agouti Netherland Dwarf. 4: Fawn Dwarf Lop. 5: Sealpoi Dwarf Lop. 6: Red-eyed White Netherland Dwarf.

Fox A coloured rabbit with a white belly.

Lilac This colour is best described as dove grey.

Opal This is an agouti colour (see above) in which each hair is slate blue at the ba gold in the centre and blue at the tip.

Otter A black, blue, chocolate or lilac-coloured rabbit with a pale beige belly with tan-coloured borders.

Sealpoint (or Siamese) Like Siamese cats (though without the blue eyes), thes rabbits have a beige-grey body with a darker grey face, ears, legs, feet and tail.

The amount of this dark shading can vary; some rabbits are dark-grey all over.

Siamese Sable This coloration, also known as Brown Sable, is the brown version of Siamese Smoke (see below). The main shade is brown – from light to very dark – while the sides, face, ears, legs, feet and tail are very dark grey.

Siamese Smoke Also known as Smoke Pearl and Blue Sable, rabbits with these markings have blue-grey fur with darker grey coloration on the sides, face, ears, legs, feet and tail.

4

5

Sooty Fawn Rabbits with this coloration, also known as Tortoiseshell or Madagascar, have an orange-brown topcoat with an underfur that is blue in tone. The sides, face, ears, legs, feet and tail are dark grey in colour.

Steel A much darker version of the agouti.

White White rabbits have either red or blue eyes. The coat should be pure white in colour.

Fancy Breeds

Fancy breed rabbits are bred to be exhibited – and, of course, to be kept as pets. Unlike Fur breeds (see pages 20–21), most Fancy breeds have never had any practical use. The exception is the Angora (see page 17), which was developed for its wool. Some of the most common and popular Fancy breeds are shown below.

Belgian Hare Although it is called a hare, and is certainly fairly large, weighir 5–5.5kg (11–12lb), this is a rabbit breed. It resembles a hare with its long body, legs and ears and its colour is usually deep re

The Belgian Hare is a specialist breed and not really suitable as a pet for a novice.

Dutch Probably the most popular pet rabbit of all, the Dutch has striking markings o white and another colour – most usually black but it ma also be blue, chocolate, yellow or tortoiseshell (sandy yellow with bla ticking). The head and ears are coloured and the face has a white blaze in the middle. Th front half of the body i white and the back coloured and half of th hind feet are white, the other half coloured. Th Dutch is quite a small breed weighing up to 2.3kg (5lb) and makes a perfect pet.

English Known in some countries as the English Spot, this is another great popular pet rabbit. It is slightly larger than the Dutch (see opposite), weighing about 2.7–3.6kg (6–8lb) and is largely white with coloured spots, coloured ears and coloured markings around the eyes. The second colour may be black, blue, tortoiseshell, chocolate or grey.

Himalayan The Himalayan is fairly small (2.kg/4.5lb) and slender with a long body. The rabbit's main colour is pure white and it has coloured – black, blue, chocolate or lilac – face, ears, feet and tail and red eyes. Thanks to its size and breeding for a good nature, it can make a good pet.

4

5

)utch 2: Belgian Hare. 3: English
-limalayan. 5: Young Lionhead (4–5 months).

Lionhead The relatively recently developed Lionhead is a friendly small breed, weighing about 1.4–1.7kg (3–3.5lb). The distinguishing feature of both males and females is a long ruff, or mane, around its neck. The rest of its coat is short.

1

Netherland Dwarf This very small rabbit, weighing no more than 0.9kg (2lb), is one of the most common breeds and comes in a wide variety of colours. However, it can be less friendly than its small size and cute appearance – it has very short ears and a round face and body – would suggest.

Polish The Polish, which is known in the USA as the Britannia Petite, takes its name not from the country, but from the glossy appearance of its coat. Although it originates from the Netherla Dwarf and is of a similar size, adults of t two breeds look nothing like each other. The Polish is slender with long legs and has a more elegant, rather than a cuddly, appearance. Polish rabbits require specialized handling and are not a good breed for beginners or children as they can be bad tempered.

2

Silver A medium-sized rabbit weighing about 1.8–2.3kg (4–5lb), the Silver can make a good pet. It is distinguished by tl silver hairs all over its body that give it a sparkling appearance. The base colour m be black (known as the Silver Grey), blue, fawn or brown.

1: Lynx Netherland Dwarf. 2: A young Polish. 3: Silver. 4: Sussex. 5: Tan.

ssex The Sussex is a medium to large abbit weighing about 3.3–3.8kg (7.5–8.5lb) nd comes in gold or cream. Developed in he 1980s in Sussex, England, it is still fairly are, but it is a good-natured and friendly reed that makes a good house rabbit.

4

ANGORA RABBITS

Angoras were originally developed for their wool and not as a Fancy breed. Their long coats are regularly shorn like that of a sheep and produce about 1kg (2.2lb) per rabbit each year. Angora rabbits need special care because of their long fur. In addition to daily grooming by their owner, they will require a special cage or hutch with a wire floor so that droppings and urine can fall through to a covered tray underneath. The Angora is therefore not a breed for those looking for a pet.

5

Tan This very attractive rabbit has a rich, deep tan underside and belly and black, blue, chocolate or lilac body. It is a medium-sized breed that doesn't require any specialized handling or grooming.

Lop-eared Rabbits

Any rabbit with ears that flop down rather than being held upright is a Lop. Lop-eared rabbits are classified as Fancy breeds and Dwarf Lops, in particular, are popular as pets. The head shape of Lop rabbits (and also of Netherland Dwarfs) puts them at high risk of serious teeth and eye problems.

2

Dwarf Lop These endearing small rabbits, with their outgoing, dog-like personalities, are among the most popular rabbit breeds kept as pets. They weigh up to 2.1 kg (4.6lb) and come in a variety of colours. As they are relatively small, they will require an experienced owner to handle them.

Unfortunately, their popularity has led to some unscrupulous breeders offering poor specimens. Check your retailer carefully and, if you can, a rabbit's background, or you could be faced with large veterinary bills later.

3

English Lop This is the oldest of all the Fancy breeds, dating back to the 1820s, and is more slender than other Lop breeds. Its extremely long ears are delicate and it will need a large hutch to help prever injury to them. For this reason, althougl it is a friendly breed, the English Lop not ideal for the beginner.

French Lop The largest of all t Lop breeds, the Frenc Lop weighs at lea 4.5kg (10lb). Its la size makes it suitable as a house rabbit but it will need a very larg hutch and run if it is to live outdoors.

1

Mini Lop The Mini Lop is thickset and firm with a cute appearance. It is quite a small rabbit, weighing up to 1.7kg (3.8lb), and so requires confident and gentle handling.

The Meissner Lop is one of the rarer Lop-eared breeds. This is a baby.

The Lionhead (see page 15) can also be combined with a Lop-eared. This young Lionhead Lop is six months old.

5

1: English Lop. 2: Mini Lop. 3: French Lop. 4: Dwarf Lop. 5: Cashmere Lop.

Cashmere Lop This relatively new and very popular breed is a long-haired version of the Dwarf Lop and, like that breed, is a popular choice as a pet. However, although its coat is not as long as that of the Angora (see page 17), it will need regular daily grooming to avoid matted fur and is therefore not recommended as a pet for beginners.

Fur Breeds

Fur breed rabbits, which are generally heavier than the Fancy breeds, were originally bred for their fur and/or their meat. Today these breeds are kept mainly as show animals and pets, though the New Zealand White is still widely used for its meat. In addition to the breeds shown here, you may see the following Fur breeds: Alaska, Argente, Beveren, Blanc de Hotot, British Giant and Californian.

Chinchilla With its silver-grey colouring and very soft, fine and dense coat, this rabbit was bred to have fur that resembled the real Chinchilla. It is a pretty breed that can also make a good pet.

Havana The dark chocolate-coloured coat of this compact breed has a dark purplish sheen and its dark eyes have a ruby glow. It is a medium-sized rabbit weighing 2.5–3kg (5.5–6.5lb) and makes a good pet.

These young Chinchilla Giganta – the giant version of the Chinchilla – are small but they are only six weeks old. Fully grown, each will weigh 4kg (9lb) or more.

New Zealand This fairly large and round rabbit, weighing 4–5.4kg (9–12lb), can make a good pet if you can handle its size. The most common colour variety is white, which has pink eyes, but the breed also comes in red, black and blue. New Zealand Whites are also bred for their meat.

Satin The coat of this medium-sized bre is exceptionally dense and fine and has a beautiful lustre. It is available in many different colours, including white, black, blue, lilac, orange, fawn, sable and smoke pearl. Many other breeds have also been developed with Satin coats.

2

3

1: New Zealand Red. 2: Satin White. 3: Silver Fox.

ilver Fox Known in the USA as the Silver Marten, this breed was developed around 1920 by crossing the Chinchilla with the Black and Tan (see page 17). Other colours – blue, lilac and chocolate – have also been developed, as well as Dwarf and Rex varieties. The Silver Fox is a medium-sized breed weighing around 2.5–3.2kg (5.5–7lb).

Rex Breeds

Rex breeds have a soft coat that is very dense. (The velvet-like texture of the Rex's coat is due to a lack of guard hairs – the longer and stronger hairs that are normally found in a rabbit's coat.) The standard Rex breed weighs 2.7–3.6kg (6–8lb) while the Mini Rex weighs 1.4–1.8kg (3–4lb).

Rex rabbits are commonly kept as pets – they are neither too small nor too large and, if handled regularly, they can become very friendly. Rexes need little grooming: any loose hairs can usually be removed by running your hands over their coat.

tip

Provide plenty of bedding

Rex breeds have thinner fur on their hocks and insufficient or sodden bedding can lead to sore hocks (see page 59).

2

1

REX COLOURS

In addition to the colours shown here, rabbits with Rex coats come in many other colours, including blue, lilac, Havana, agouti (known as Castor Rex), sealpoint, fox, tan, harlequin, tri-colour and Himalayan. The white (shown opposite) is known as the Ermine Rex.

moke Pearl Rex 2: Ermine Rex.
Dalmation Rex. 4: Black Rex.
Orange Rex. 6: Sable Rex.

5 6

Housing Your Rabbit

Providing suitable accommodation outside or indoors

Rabbits are active creatures and so need plenty of room to move. How big your new pet's living quarters need to be will depend partly on which breed you have chosen. Don't forget that your new pet may not yet be fully grown. The hutch or cage you choose will need to be tall enough for your rabbit to stand on its hind legs and long enough for it to stretch out in comfort and take three or four hops in any given direction when it has reached its full adult size.

Outside or indoors?

The type of hutch or cage you choose for your rabbit will also depend on where you plan to house it. Traditionally, rabbits have been kept outdoors in a hutch, but they also make good indoor pets and they can be house trained. A house rabbit, which may be given the run of a house, like a cat or dog, will still need to be provided with a suitable cage or hutch. This will give it a base to which it can retire when it wants some privacy, or in which you can shut it when necessary.

QUIPMENT CHECKLIST

efore you buy your new rabbit you will need to make sure that you have suitable commodation – and all other essential equipment – ready for it. In addition to the ems below, you will need to provide an exercise run (see page 46).

Cleaning materials

he hutch will need cleaning gularly and it is important o use only pet-fe disinfectant.

Food
(see pages 38–41)

Buy food at the same time as you buy your rabbit so that it has the food it is used to.

Water bottle

One that attaches to the sides of the hutch or cage is best.

Wood shavings
(see pages 28–29)

You will need a good supply to line the hutch.

Hay rack
(see page 39)

Choose one that vill attach to the side of the hutch or cage.

Hutch
(see pages 26–27)

Make sure it is big enough and that it has a bedding area. If you want to keep your rabbit indoors, provide a suitable cage (see pages 30–31).

Food bowls
(see page 38)

You will need to buy at least two – one for dried food and one for fresh food items.

Straw
(see page 28–29)

A necessary additional bedding material, particularly for a rabbit housed out of doors.

The Hutch – housing a rabbit outside

If you provide plenty of warm bedding and choose a suitable site, the rabbit hutch can be kept outside all year round. Choose a good-quality one that will be able to withstand adverse weather conditions. If it has not been pre-treated, you will need to weatherproof it, but make sure that you use a preservative that is non-toxic to animals.

In winter you can place the hutch in a well-ventilated shed or outbuilding. Indeed, if you have a light, airy shed available, it is no bad thing to keep the hutch under cover all year round – then you won't be tempted to put off cleaning out the cage just because it's raining!

If your rabbit is going to live undercover all year round, you can use a hutch of a more simple construction – it won't need a sloping roof and it can be made of plywood (though it's still a good idea to treat it with wood preservative).

Whether you keep your rabbit an outdoor hutch or in your h you will also need to provide with a safe enclosure in which can run around outside.

MINIMUM HUTCH SIZES

The following are the minimum sizes of hutch recommended for different sized breeds. It makes sense, however, to choose as large a hutch as you can afford and have space for. Don't forget to check the height of the cage – a rabbit should be able to stand on its hind legs without its head touching the roof.

Small breed e.g. Netherland Dwarf, Dwarf Lop 90x60cm (36x24in)

Medium- to large-sized breed e.g. English 120x60cm (48x24in)

Giant breed e.g. French Lop, New Zealand 150x60cm (60x24in)

A SUITABLE HUTCH

A sloping roof will ensure that rainwater can drain off.

The separate sleeping compartment has its own door. Check that the opening between the two areas of the cage is large enough.

The living area is covered by a mesh door. Choose a hutch with doors that open outwards rather than up or down.

Wood shavings provide suitable bedding material and can be covered with a thick layer of straw.

The hutch should be raised on legs to protect it and its occupants from damp.

his is another d sturdy cage gn, though as ainwater may ool on its flat oof, it may be etter located der cover in a large shed.

Locating the hutch

Rabbits prefer colder conditions to warm ones but they will not withstand a wet hutch. Choose a sheltered spot where your rabbit will be protected from rain and from direct sunlight. If possible, place the hutch with its back against a house or outbuilding for maximum protection but allow a gap for airflow, as rabbits still need ventilation.

In very bad weather the front of the hutch can be covered with tarpaulin, but make sure that you leave a gap so that your rabbit has an adequate air supply. Remember to lift the cover as soon as the sun comes out to prevent the temperature inside the hutch from rising too high.

If you are keeping the hutch in a shed or outbuilding, make sure that there is plenty of ventilation and enough space for you to access the hutch to clean it out. Never locate the hutch in a garage where cars are kept.

Bedding materials

The hutch will need to be lined with suitable bedding materials. Use a layer o wood shavings on the bottom of the ca to soak up wet patches and top this wit

Rabbits appreciate plenty of straw, particularly if they are housed outside, when it will provide extra warmth.

Make sure that the wire mesh on the hutch ɔor is strong and securely attached to keep out predators such as dogs, cats and foxes.

tip

Buy wood shavings from a pet store

Pet stores sell wood shavings that are safe for use with pets; those from other sources may have been made from wood that has been treated with poisonous preservatives.

DETERRING VERMIN

The wire mesh on the front of a rabbit hutch needs to be small-gauge to keep out mice, which can squeeze through larger holes in search of food and will spread disease.

Make sure that your rabbit's food is stored in strong, waterproof containers with securely fitting lids and always replace these. Keep the shed clean and sweep up any food spillages in the area promptly.

a generous amount of straw. Although you can use wood shavings on their own, they can get tangled up in the rabbit's fur.

Don't use newspaper, as your rabbit will tear it into pieces making a very untidy hutch. Also, the ink in the newspaper may stain the fur of pale-coloured rabbits. Never use sawdust as this is too fine and can seriously injure your rabbit if it gets into its nostrils or eyes.

BREEDING CAGES

If you want to keep several rabbits, you will need to house them separately so that they have enough space to move around comfortably and to prevent fighting. Rabbit breeders, who need large numbers of cages, use special breeding hutches in blocks. From specialist manufacturers you can buy from as few as two hutch compartments to as many as 24 and they are available in varying sizes.

The Cage – housing a rabbit indoors

If you want to keep a rabbit indoors, you will need to think about how much freedom you are going to allow it in the house. Some owners give their rabbit a cage to live in most of the time; others will allow their pet to roam around the house unsupervised.

You may decide to use a hutch similar to an outdoor one – it can be made from plywood and won't need a sloping roof or you can provide your pet with a simp indoor cage. Whichever form of accommodation you decide upon, your rabbit will need an area that it can go t for privacy as well as enough space to r around – whether that's within its living quarters or around the house (see The House Rabbit, pages 48–49).

A SUITABLE INDOOR CAGE

A water bottle is easily attached to the side of the cage.

Two separate access hatches means that you can retrieve your rabbit wherever it is in the cage. Make sure the catches are secure.

A deep plastic base will help prevent straw and other bedding materials falling out of the cage and is easy to clean out.

The plastic-coated wire canopy is easy to lift off the base when you need to clean the cage.

A hay rack is useful to prevent hay from being trampled and soiled. It allows the rabbit to pull down what it wants to eat at the time, keeping the rest safe for later.

There is plenty of space in this indoor play pen, but make sure you provide somewhere private for your rabbit to use as a bedding area.

This indoor home for a house rabbit is spacious and secure and the rabbit can use the deep tray lined with straw as a bedding area.

tip Rabbit-proof your home

Prevent your house rabbit from chewing wires, wallpaper and carpets by providing it with lots of hay. Rabbit-proof your home (see page 48) before you allow it to hop around freely.

Most house rabbits can be persuaded to use a litter tray filled with wood shavings.

Buying Your Rabbit

Deciding what to buy and choosing a healthy individual

Before you rush off to your local pet shop to choose a new rabbit, you will need to make sure not only that you have its home ready (see chapter 3), but also that you have thought about exactly what sort of rabbit you are going to buy.

Have you considered the different breeds and which might be suitable (see chapter 2)? It is never a good idea to be seduced by the cuddly appearance of a young rabbit in a pet shop if it might grow into a large animal with special needs that you have neither the space to accommodate nor the experience to handle.

If you decide to keep two rabbits, make sure that you have enough space.

ıe rabbit or two?

ʀabbits need company, but a male ınd female sharing a hutch will breed – ıon-stop – while two males may fight. ˉwo young females may live together ›eacefully, especially if they are sisters, ›ut are likely to become territorial and ıggressive once they reach maturity.

The only really safe solution, if you ʋant to keep two rabbits ogether, is to have a male ınd female and take them o a vet to have them ıeutered. You will need o neuter both rabbits ›r the one with ıormones intact may ›ully its companion.

Ɔne rabbit will live happily on own provided ıat you give it plenty of attention a daily basis.

Male or female?

Individuals of either sex can make good pets, but a buck (male) is often a better choice as bucks generally have a more even temperament and are more playful, while sexually mature does (females) can often become territorial and aggressive. However, bucks are more likely to spray urine as a territorial marker and some may develop the habit of mounting an owner's arm or leg. Having a buck neutered should prevent it spraying, calm it down and might improve a bad temper.

Adult or baby?

The ideal age is to buy a young rabbit is when it is about eight weeks old and it should be accustomed to being handled. A rabbit younger than this will be too immature and a good pet shop won't try to offer you babies. Animal charities and rescue centres will have older rabbits in need of a home. Such animals may take longer to train, however, particularly if they have been neglected in the past.

These baby rabbits are still much too young to leave home.

tip

Buy a youngster for a house rabbit

While, in theory, any breed can be house-trained, it's always easiest to start with a young rabbit.

The Right Pet – choosing it and taking it home

Having decided what sort of rabbit you would like to buy, you need to find a suitable retailer. Don't feel pressured into making a quick decision, but take time to look at the condition of the cages and animals and question staff. (Be sensitive to the fact that they may have less time to devote to you on a busy weekend.)

Check that cages are clean and that the rabbits on display have food and clean water. The animals should appear generally lively and confident.

Selecting a healthy individual

If you have found a good retailer, you can begin to select an individual rabbit. Look for one that is alert and has bright eyes and soft shiny fur. Ask the retailer to get the rabbit out of its cage so that you can inspect it closely. This may give you an idea of the rabbit's temperament as well as its physical condition.

Taking your rabbit home

You may want to have a basket or cage which to transport your new rabbit hom (though a pet shop should provide a special box) and it's a good idea to buy this before you purchase your rabbit. Yc can also use the carrying case for taking your pet to the vet and for keeping it sa while you clean its cage.

Always try to make sure that you have the opportunity tc handle a rabbi yourself before you make a decision to choose it.

CHOOSING A HEALTHY RABBIT

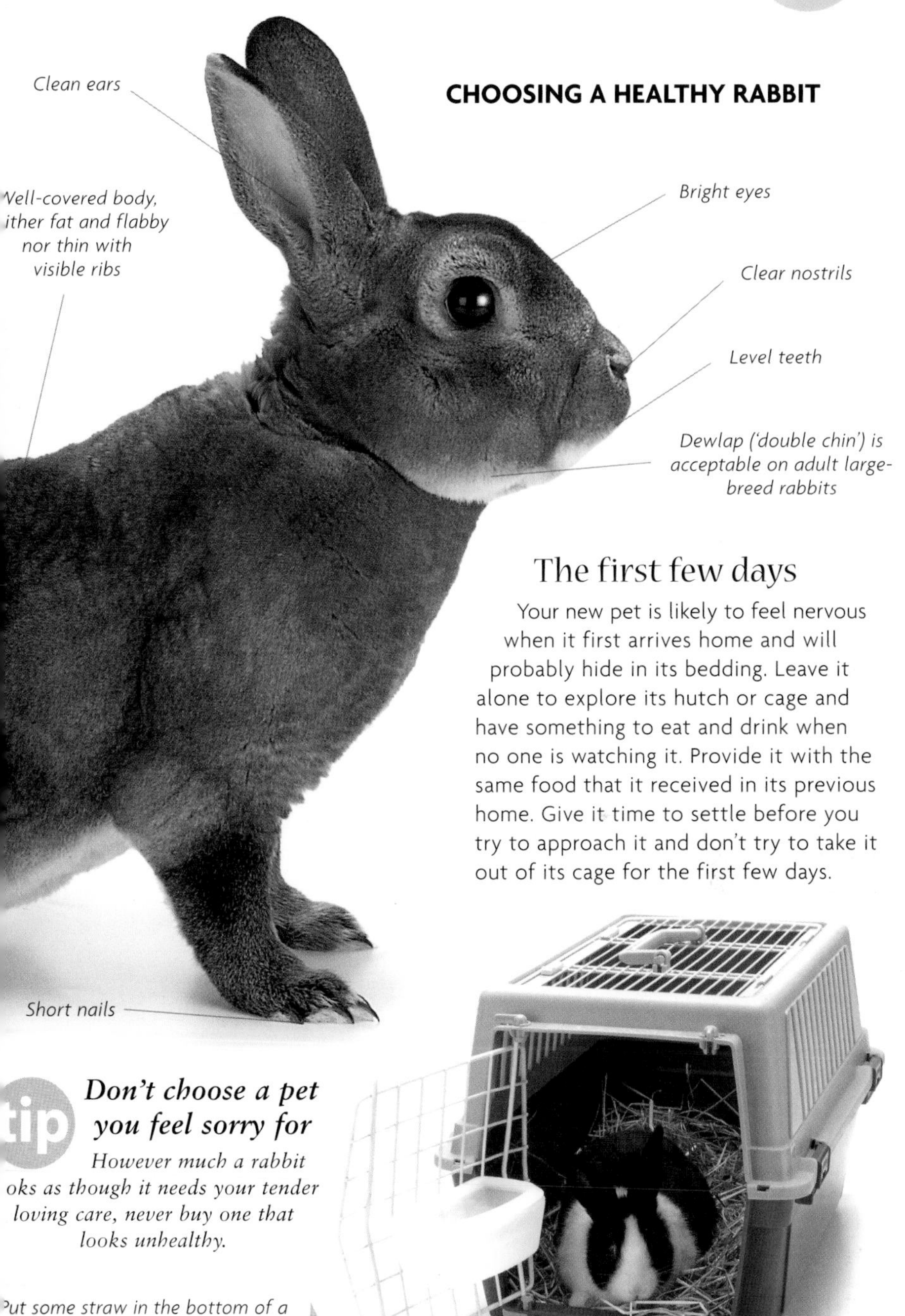

The first few days

Your new pet is likely to feel nervous when it first arrives home and will probably hide in its bedding. Leave it alone to explore its hutch or cage and have something to eat and drink when no one is watching it. Provide it with the same food that it received in its previous home. Give it time to settle before you try to approach it and don't try to take it out of its cage for the first few days.

tip ***Don't choose a pet you feel sorry for***

However much a rabbit oks as though it needs your tender loving care, never buy one that looks unhealthy.

ʾut some straw in the bottom of a carrying case so that your rabbit will feel more secure in transit.

Caring for Your Rabbit

Enjoying your rabbit and keeping it healthy

Rabbits are not particularly high-maintenance pets but, in order to keep your new pet healthy and friendly, you will need to spend some time every day caring for it. Providing your rabbit with a good, balanced diet and keeping its hutch or cage clean is obviously a priority, but spending time with your rabbit every day is just as important. Rabbits are sociable animals and your new pet will need your company, particularly if it is to become tame. Spending time examining it will also help to ensure that you spot any potential health problems before they develop.

Stick to a routine

tip *You will find it helpful to establish regular routines for caring for your rabbit and keeping its hutch or cage clean. Make a note of when you perform these tasks to remind you of when they are next due.*

You should be able to feel your rabbit's hips and ribs with your fingers but they should not be sticking out.

Get used to the feel as well as the appearance of your rabbit. You can check for any lumps and bumps and feel whether your pet is too fat or thin whenever you pick it up.

ROUTINE MAINTENANCE TASKS

Daily
- Remove any uneaten perishable food.
- Check the water bottle for any leaks or blockages and wash out food bowls.
- Feed your rabbit and provide clean water (see pages 38–41).
- Take your rabbit out of the cage to give it some attention and exercise.
- Check that your rabbit's eyes and ears are clean (see page 55).
- Remove and replace any soiled bedding.

Weekly
- Clean out the hutch or cage, discarding and replacing wood shavings and straw.
- Check for any damage to the hutch or cage and its furnishings.
- Check your rabbit's nails: make sure that they are short with no splits (see page 54).
- Groom the rabbit to prevent its coat becoming matted (see page 52–53).
- Scrub out the water bottle.
- Weigh your rabbit (see page 57).

Monthly
- Wash the base of the hutch or cage using a pet-safe disinfectant (see pages 50–51).
- Check the rabbit's teeth (see pages 54–55).

Feeding – providing a balanced diet

Rabbits have sensitive stomachs and it is important that you don't make sudden changes to their diet. Before you buy your rabbit, find out what sort of diet it has been fed on and buy the same mix. Introduce a diet change gradually by mixing the old food and the new food at first. The majority of the rabbit's diet must be good-quality hay with a small amount of pellet food or a concentrated mix as well as some green food (for example cabbage leaves).

A water bottle clipped to the front of the hutch or cage avoids risks of spillage or fouling of the water.

In addition to supplying your rabbit with food, don't forget to ensure that it has fresh water available at all times. Although rabbits that eat some fresh food (such as greens) will drink less than those on a dried food diet, they will still need to have water available to them.

Feeding routine

Your rabbit will need feeding once a day and it doesn't matter too much when this is, though rabbits do most of their eating during the early part of the morning or evening. Try to keep to a regular time each day: this way you

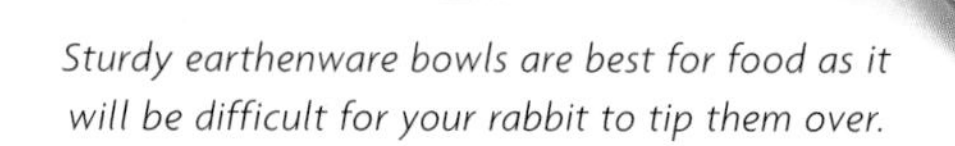

Sturdy earthenware bowls are best for food as it will be difficult for your rabbit to tip them over.

Find out what diet your new pet has been fed on before you buy it and stick to that initially. Sudden changes in diet, particularly for young rabbits, can be fatal.

will learn your rabbit's routine and will notice if your pet is not eating or drinking.

How much you feed will depend on the size of the breed. If your rabbit seems hungry, you can increase the amount a little; if your pet is getting too fat, then reduce the portion size.

upplying hay

Hay forms an essential part of a rabbit's diet by providing roughage so make sure that it is always available. Your pet shop will sell suitable hay in plastic bags, but it is best to transfer it into another container where air can circulate.

Supply the hay to your rabbit in a special hay rack rather than leaving it on the floor of the hutch or cage where it will soon become soiled. Avoid using hay that is dusty or smells musty.

Rabbit mixes and pellets

In addition to hay, a proprietary rabbit mix or pellets will form a complete diet for your pet. There are many different mixes available but make sure that you choose one that is specifically produced for rabbits. A good-quality one will contain equal amounts of oats, barley, pellets and flakes of dried peas and maize. Avoid sweetened mixes or any that contain coloured biscuits. Make sure that your rabbit eats all of its food and does not pick out just the bits that it likes.

Pellets lack variety, but are produced to contain all the nutritional elements that a rabbit needs so they prevent selective feeding and are therefore highly recommended.

tip

Store dry food in solid containers

Make sure that food containers have sealed lids and that you replace them to avoid contamination of the food by mice and other vermin.

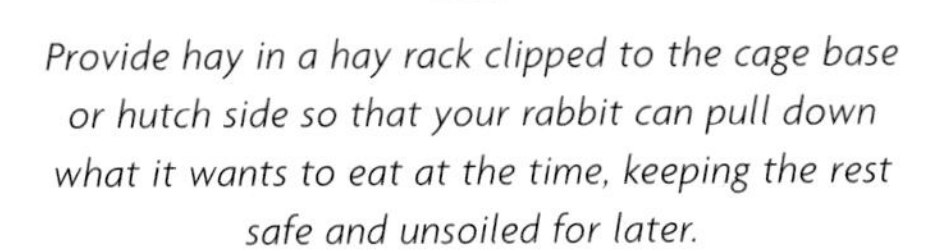

Provide hay in a hay rack clipped to the cage base or hutch side so that your rabbit can pull down what it wants to eat at the time, keeping the rest safe and unsoiled for later.

Your rabbit will enjoy some fresh food in its diet, but introduce such food slowly and limit its intake.

Green foods

If your rabbit's outdoor run is put on a fresh patch of lawn every day, it will have a ready supply of green food, but in winter, when it may be too cold or wet to go on the lawn, you will need to feed a few more green vegetables.

Rabbits enjoy some fresh food, particularly greens, in their diet, but too much may cause tummy upsets and diarrhoea. If your pet isn't used to fresh food, introduce it slowly and always ensure that it is fresh and washed in clea water. Popular vegetables include green cabbage, broccoli, carrot, baby sweetcor peas and spinach. Lettuce is not recommended for rabbits as it contains a chemical that can induce tiredness and make the rabbit appear unwell. You coul also try feeding a small piece of apple, pear, tomato, melon or a single strawber but only as a rare treat.

SUITABLE WILD FOOD

Something to chew

Unlike our teeth, the teeth of rabb grow and need to be worn down by continual grazing. To ensure that they don't become overgrow you should make sure that your rabbit ha something appropriate to chew. Providing hay as the main bulk of the rabbit's diet will prevent many problems. A commercially available chew block, or length of branch, may also help to encourage your rabbit to chew. Wood from any fruit tree should be suitable, provided it has not been sprayed with pesticides.

DANGEROUS PLANTS

Some common garden plants can prove fatal if your rabbit eats them. The following list is not exhaustive: many bulbs are also poisonous.

- Anemones
- Elder
- Figwort
- Foxgloves
- Poppies
- Nightshade
- Wild clematis

tip ***Feed treats sparingly***

Like humans, rabbits suffer from obesity if they eat too many treats, particularly if they are sweetened.

reats and supplements

Hand-feeding your rabbit titbits is a great way to help it gain confidence in you, but too many treats – particularly sweet ones – will lead to obesity. The occasional commercial or carbohydrate treat is fine, but it is best to stick to healthy snacks such as pieces of vegetable. Never feed snacks meant for humans to your rabbit.

If your rabbit has a balanced diet, it should not need supplements.

If your rabbit is 'sed to green food, you don't need to remove the leaves from the branches 'rovided you check 'hat the leaves are not poisonous.

Handling and Taming Your Rabbit

For the first few days, a new rabbit will be quite shy and may not come out of its sleeping quarters while you are around. It will take a while for your rabbit to become accustomed to you – remember that your pet will have all the instincts of its wild ancestors, which are prey animals, hunted by other species. Make time to spend with it every day and it will soon become tame enough to trust you to pick it up and cuddle it.

Offering your rabbit a food treat will help it gain confidence in you. Once your rabbit is happily nibbling the treat, you can start to stroke your pet gently.

First approaches

Don't try to pick your rabbit up at first. For a few days, leave it in its cage and just talk to it gently. Once it has ventured out of its nest box, try offering it some food, such as a small piece of carrot or apple – it may be brave enough to take it from your hand. Move slowly and don't put your fingers near its mouth or it may nip you – it will take a while for your pet to recognize your smell. Try not to loom

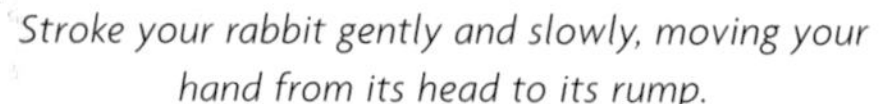

Stroke your rabbit gently and slowly, moving your hand from its head to its rump.

over your rabbit when you approach it (you may have to lift the hutch higher off the floor and sit on the floor in front of the hutch).

If your pet seems comfortable, you can begin to stroke it, but keep your hands away from its nose. Be aware of your rabbit's body language (see page 9) and respect when it is frightened or has just had enough. Until it is confident with you, don't force yourself upon your pet, but let it make the advances.

tip

Be patient with a nervous rabbit

A rabbit that was not handled regularly as a baby may be nervous when it first comes to live with you. Don't force your pet to be handled, but gradually build up its confidence using treats and a calm tone of voice. Never tell your pet off if it is aggressive, as this will make it more scared of you.

icking up your rabbit

Rabbits are ground-dwellers and can become anxious when held above ground level. (In the wild this would only happen if they were caught by a predator.) Most rabbits will be nervous at first and some will never feel comfortable being carried around, but many will learn to accept being carried.

Never pick up your rabbit by its ears: this will be painful for the rabbit and can damage muscles and ear membranes. The best way to pick up your pet is to put one hand round its chest behind the forelegs and, as you lift it up, support its rump with the other hand. Bring your rabbit against your body, keeping it supported. When it is more confident, you can hold it sideways on for comfort and eventually it will snuggle down in your arms and enjoy the experience.

Support your rabbit below and on both sides so that it feels safe and secure.

Staying safe

Rabbits that are unused to handling will wriggle and kick out. Remember that your rabbit may not mean to hurt you, it just wants to escape. Nevertheless, its hind legs are strong and can kick hard and its forelegs, though weaker, still have sharp claws that can scratch you painfully. To avoid getting hurt, it is wise to take a few precautions while you and your rabbit are learning to trust each other. Keep your pet's legs aimed away from you and never pick it up when you have bare arms.

When you first pick up your new rabbit, it will prefer to be held on your lap than to be carried around. Sit with your pet on your lap, stroke it gently and speak to it calmly.

UNDERSTANDING AGGRESSIVE BEHAVIOUR

Aggression – demonstrated by grunting, pouncing and biting – may be directed towards you or other rabbits. The most likely cause is fear: it will take a little time for a new rabbit to become accustomed to you and settle into its new home. If you have acquired a rabbit that has been neglected in the past, it is likely to be more than usually fearful and therefore may tend to display aggressive behaviour.

Your rabbit may also be defending its food or territory – a nursing doe will fiercely defend her young, for example. False pregnancy is not uncommon (see page 63) and can also lead to aggressive behaviour. If you have only one rabbit, or a neutered pair, such behaviour is less likely to be a problem.

If your rabbit does seem to be scared of you, roll your hands in some of its dirty bedding first and then approach it from the side rather than from the front. Make sure that you stay safe by handling your rabbit carefully (see opposite).

If food aggression seems to be the problem, it may help to provide several food sources. Your rabbit is likely to be less territorial if it is able to graze on hay and green foods than if it receives just a bowl full of pellets.

Miniature breeds such as Netherland Dwarfs can be more nervous than larger breeds and therefore require confident handling to prevent problems developing.

Rabbits can be nervous and your pet may feel safer being carried around in a basket or bucket than in your arms.

Stay low

To a rabbit, humans are huge. It will be easier to win your rabbit's confidence if you get down to its level.

Exercise Outdoors – safety in the garde

Rabbits need a lot of exercise – more than they can get if they are kept in a hutch all day – and even if your rabbit has space to run around indoors, it needs fresh air. An exercise run is essential whether you keep your pet outside or indoors. Choose one that is covered so that your rabbit can't escape. Ideally it should have a sheltered area at one end so that your rabbit can have some privacy and shelter from the sun. Put some straw in this area so that your pet feels secure.

The exercise run can be moved around the garden. Make sure your pet can retreat from the sun if it needs to.

Outside the run

Giving your pet free run of the garden is advisable only if you are certain that the garden is completely escape-proof and that there are no poisonous plants. Even then, you should supervise your pet's play time in case a stray dog, cat or fox jumps over the fence.

A lightweight nylon rabbit harness can provide a useful safety restraint for pottering around the garden, but make sure that it fits well and don't pull your rabbit along. Don't try to take your rabbi for a walk in the park as you would a do though – it is best to keep them away from animals that might try to chase the and sounds that might scare them.

Always supervise your rabbit if you leave it loose to run around the garden.

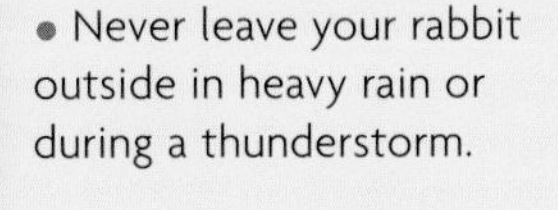

Don't chase your rabbit

Two rabbits may play chase games, but don't join in – playing chase with humans will feel too much like being hunted for your rabbit.

Make sure that a harness fits securely but not tightly.

SAFETY IN THE GARDEN

- Make sure that the run is partially covered so that your rabbit is shaded from hot sun and protected from sudden rain.
- Always supervise a rabbit left outside and make sure that the garden is completely escape-proof before you let your rabbit loose.
- Ensure that your rabbit doesn't have access to poisonous plants.
- Check the grass for anything sharp that might harm your rabbit.
- Never leave your rabbit outside in heavy rain or during a thunderstorm.

IF YOUR RABBIT GETS WET

A wet rabbit is a chilled rabbit. If your pet gets very wet, gently towel-dry its fur as much as possible, then keep it indoors in a box full of straw until it has thoroughly dried out.

Rabbits feel safer if some shelter is available to them – flowerpots or cardboard boxes are good for playing hide and seek.

The House Rabbit – safety in the hom

Keeping a rabbit as a house pet – in the same way as a dog or cat – is not new and any rabbit can be trained to live indoors, even one that has previously been kept outside. Bear in mind that rabbits enjoy chewing and scratching, however. As well as making sure that any room that you allow your rabbit access to is free from potential hazards – fires, electrical wires etc. – you will need to make sure you remove anything you don' want to be damaged.

Make sure you cover any furniture in the room that you don't want your rabbit to damage.

House-training

Most rabbits can be house-trained like a cat. Place some wood shavings or a non-clumping cat litter into a plastic tray along with some of your rabbit's dirty litter. Clean the tray out every few days, but put back just a bit of dirty bedding until your rabbit is fully toilet trained. If your rabbit can detect its own smell in the tray, it will toilet in the same place. I the tray is too clean, your rabbit may no learn to toilet within the tray.

RABBIT-PROOFING YOUR HOUSE

Make sure you have dealt with the following hazards before allowing your rabbit loose in the house.

- Tidy the room of clutter.
- Cover a fireplace with a secure guard.
- Place any houseplants on a high table out of reach.
- Ensure that all electrical wires are out of reach.
- Cover any furniture you don't want damaged.
- Keep doors shut and let other people in the house know your pet is loose in the room so they don't open them suddenly.
- Keep other pets and very young children out of the room.
- Shorten floor-length curtains, or tie them up above rabbit level.

A solid plastic ball is a useful and inexpensive toy that your rabbit will enjoy nosing around.

Other pets

Although cats and dogs are a rabbit's natural enemies, they may learn to accept each other if they are brought up together. It is important to introduce them slowly, however, keeping the rabbit within its hutch or indoor cage, and you should always monitor their time together.

Rabbits naturally enjoy tunnelling and your pet will enjoy exploring a piece of drainpipe.

ogs and rabbits :an get on, but need to be introduced to 'ch other slowly and carefully.

Play time

Rabbits are playful creatures, especially bucks, and racing around, jumping and leaping are natural ways for a healthy rabbit to burn off surplus energy. Offering attractive toys and plenty of hay to your rabbit will make play times more interesting and will help prevent it chewing forbidden alternatives.

tip

Supervise play time

It is a good idea to keep a young rabbit, in particular, in a cage for most of the day and to supervise its play time in the house.

Hutch Hygiene – routine care

A clean and dry hutch is essential to your rabbit's wellbeing and the best way to ensure this is to do some housekeeping every day. Rabbits are territorial and your pet may not appreciate your efforts – as far as it is concerned, you are simply barging into its home and rearranging the furniture! It is best to give your rabbit some food or a treat to keep it occupied while you have a tidy up. It may express its objections by deliberately getting in your way and even nipping you. Be patient and it will soon become accustomed to the routine.

Daily housekeeping

Remove wet bedding from the hutch an clear heavily soiled areas daily, replacing with fresh wood shavings and straw. Remove any uneaten fresh food and was and dry the bowls before refilling them. Wash and refill the water bottle, checki for any leakages and blockages.

tip

Compost hutch-cleanings

Rather than disposing of hutch-cleanings with household waste, add them to a compost heap – they produce an excellent material for soil improvement.

A WEEKLY CLEANING ROUTINE

1 Once a week the cage should be cleaned thoroughly. Place your rabbit in its exercise run or carrying cage, remove everything from the cage and brush it out.

utch safety

When you are cleaning out your rabbit's hutch, check for areas that may have become damaged. Problems are best picked up early before any real harm ensues.

Your rabbit may have started chewing the timber: make sure that you do any necessary repair work before a big hole develops and give your pet something more suitable to chew on.

Check your rabbit's cage regularly for sharp edges of wire, chewed holes, loose door catches and rotting wood.

If you have not aired the hutch weekly, you may find that urine may has soaked through the bedding in a corner, making the wood soggy and likely to rot and this corner will need attention. (Supply extra bedding and clean the hutch regularly or provide your rabbit with a litter tray in this area.)

Sometimes wire mesh can work loose, leaving dangerous sharp edges that could cause injury. Check that door catches are secure too.

2 In summer, scrub the hutch out with hot soapy water, paying special attention to the orners. Rinse it well and allow the hutch to dry ut thoroughly. In winter, wet cage cannot dry in the sun so substitute a light wipe-over with a mild, pet-safe disinfectant.

3 Add plenty of fresh bedding materials, including a little soiled bedding in the toilet area so that your rabbit feels at home.

Provide a litter tray

Placing a small litter tray in the toilet area of your rabbit's hutch will make it easier to keep the hutch clean.

Grooming and Checks – for good healt

In addition to keeping your rabbit's cage clean and providing it with fresh food and water daily, you will also need to give it some regular attention. This means not only playing with your pet but also grooming its coat – particularly if you have a long-haired breed – and checking that it is in good health. Establishing a weekly health check routine will ensure that you pick up any potential problems before they develop into something serious.

Coat care

Rabbits take good care of their own coa and short-haired breeds can groom themselves, using their teeth and claws combs. Giving your rabbit a weekly gent groom with a soft brush or slicker brush will remove any surplus dead hair and will help to develop your relationship with your pet. It will also give you the opportunity to make a regula check on

Even a short-haired rabbit will benefit fr a weekly brushing.

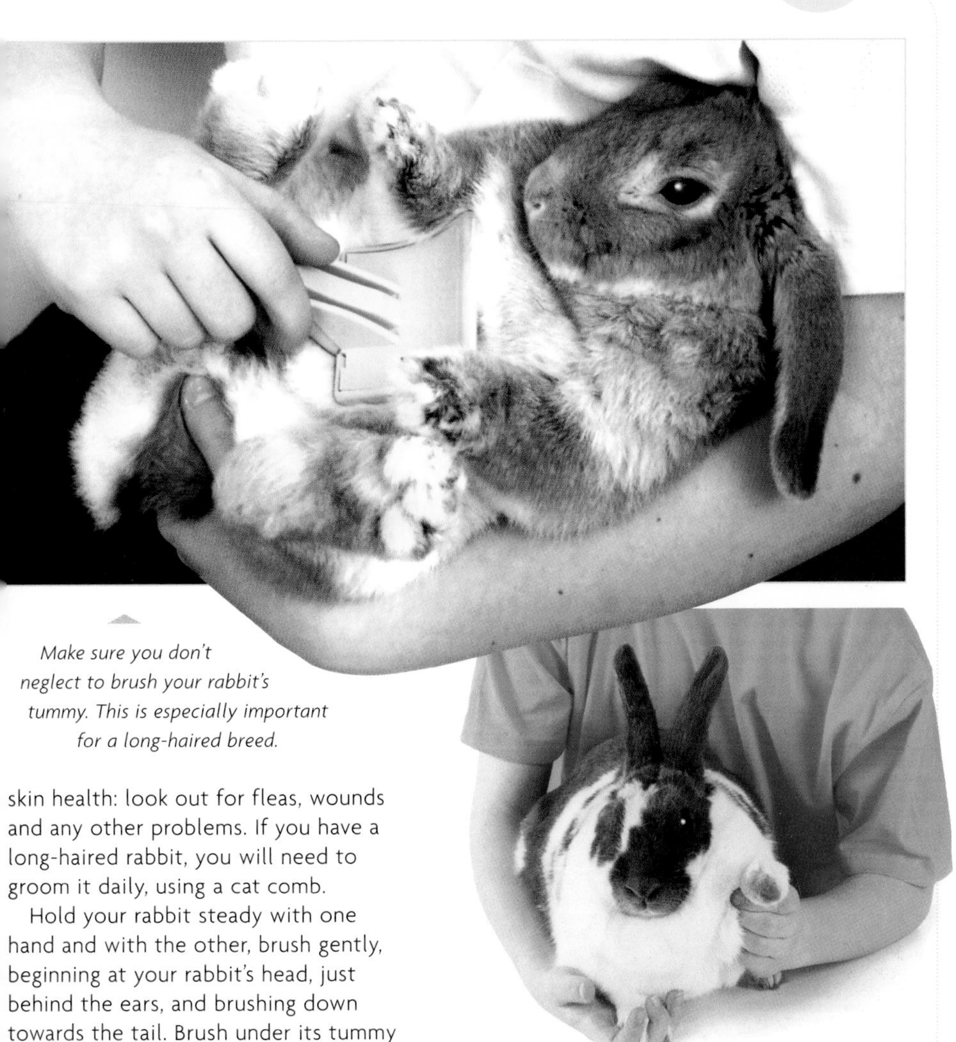

Make sure you don't neglect to brush your rabbit's tummy. This is especially important for a long-haired breed.

skin health: look out for fleas, wounds and any other problems. If you have a long-haired rabbit, you will need to groom it daily, using a cat comb.

Hold your rabbit steady with one hand and with the other, brush gently, beginning at your rabbit's head, just behind the ears, and brushing down towards the tail. Brush under its tummy too – it may wriggle. Sometimes the fur between a rabbit's toes can become matted so check its feet as well.

Check your rabbit's feet and nails and remove any droppings that have become stuck in the fur.

MOULTING

Wild rabbits moult twice a year to shed their winter and summer coats but pet rabbits vary: if your rabbit lives indoors in a centrally heated house, it may moult continuously or not at all.

A moult can be very heavy – you may find the hutch full of shed fur. Groom your pet daily while it is moulting and make sure you remove dead hair from its hutch.

Clipping nails

As well as checking between your rabbit's toes for matted fur, you will need to make sure that its nails have not become overgrown. If left to overgrow, a rabbit's nails will be more likely to scratch you and, more importantly, may curve round

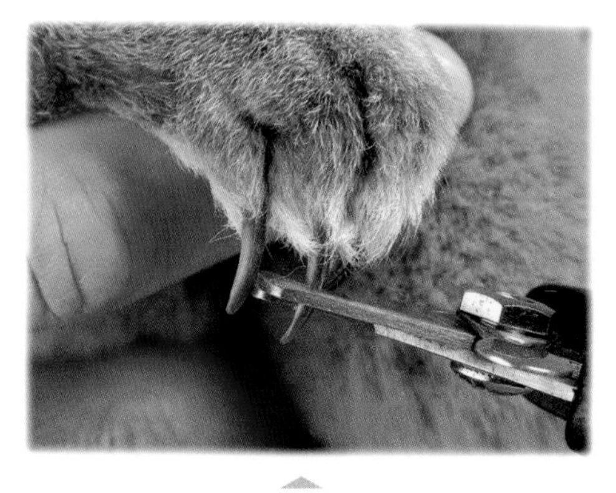

Overgrown claws make walking and grooming difficult for your rabbit.

and grow into the rabbit's paw, which will be very painful for your pet.

Ask your vet to show you how to clip your rabbit's nails if you have not done this before. If you cut them too short, you will cause pain and bleeding. If the claws are

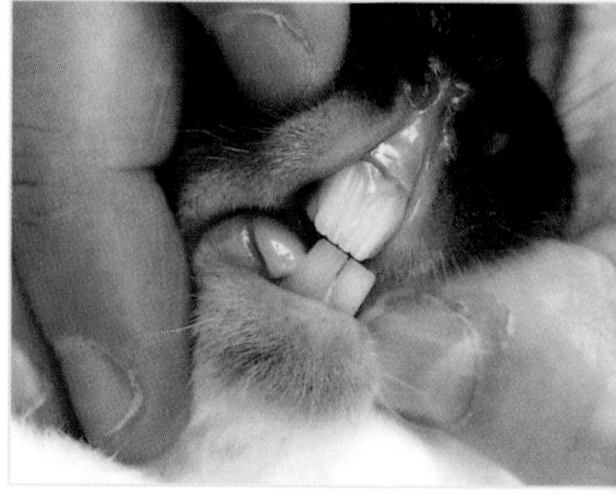

Check your rabbit's teeth weekly to make sure that have not overgrown.

white, it will be easy to see the pink 'quic and cut above this, but with dark claws you need to be more careful. If you make mistake, press the injured claw into a dan bar of soap to stop the bleeding.

Checking teeth

If a rabbit lacks the opportunity to chew regularly, has a poor diet or has inheritec dental problems, teeth can grow too long, making eating difficult.

Check your pet's teeth as part of your weekly health routine. Warning signs include dribbling, over-grooming and eating problems. If your rabbit's teeth do grow too long, they will need attention from your vet.

You can clean the inside of your rabbit's ears carefully with a hygiene pet wipe.

ars, eyes and nose

Healthy ears are clean and almost wax-free. If your rabbit's ears are hot, dirty, smelly or wax-filled, your pet may have an infection, which will require veterinary attention. The long, folded ears of Lop breeds are particularly vulnerable as they provide a warm, dark environment that is an ideal home for parasites.

The nose should be clean and free of discharge – snuffles and sneezes can mean potentially fatal diseases. Eyes should be clear and bright. Watering eyes may mean an infection or an injury and can also be a sign of dental problems.

nder your rabbit's tail

The first set of faeces produced by rabbits are wet and smelly and are normally eaten by the rabbit (you may see them do this from time to time) and the second set are drier and harder. The first set will attract flies if the faeces have got stuck on the rabbit's bottom and this can result in 'fly strike'– flies lay eggs on the soiled fur and the maggots that hatch out will literally eat the rabbit alive. Good hutch hygiene reduces the risk, but it is worth inspecting your rabbit's bottom daily.

Overweight rabbits are very likely to leave faeces around their bottom area because they are not able to reach round and remove them. In addition faeces can get trapped in the fur of longhaired rabbits, particularly if the rabbit is not groomed daily.

s of hay, as well as a toy or branch on which your bbit can chew will help keep its teeth in check as ell as distract it from chewing unsuitable objects.

tip

Prevention is better than cure!

Don't neglect a weekly health check – it could save your rabbit from unnecessary discomfort and you from expensive vet's bills.

Health Care – symptoms and cures

The most common causes of disease in rabbits are a poor diet and dirty living quarters. If you care for your rabbit properly and don't neglect regular housekeeping and health checks (see pages 50–55), your pet should live for five to seven years or more.

No matter how well you look after your rabbit, however, it may sometimes become ill so it is important that you learn to spot symptoms and provide prompt treatment. Many treatments can be purchased over the counter and administered at home, but if you are in any doubt, it is always best to consult a vet.

What to look for

A sick rabbit is usually lethargic and will stay hunched at the back of its hutch rather than coming out to greet you. It will lose its appetite and its fur may lack its usual lustre. Droppings are a good indication of health – most should be neat, hard balls. Lots of soft droppings or a lack of droppings indicate a problem (see page 59).

A weekly weigh-in is another good way of monitoring your pet's health. The scales may show a change of

Learn to recognize the normal appearance, feel and behaviour of your rabbit and you will quickly be able to spot and deal with anything unusual.

Your rabbit will need to become accustomed to being weighed before it will sit still.

weight before you would notice it otherwise. Keep a record of weight loss or gain week by week so that you can see any patterns emerging. Any sudden weight change needs investigation.

Wounds and injuries

If you have two rabbits living together and they fight, you will need to separate them immediately and check for any wounds. Any injuries should be looked at by a veterinary surgeon. Although most wounds will be caused by bites from another rabbit, your pet may injure itself in other ways, particularly if it has free run of a garden or house. It is important to clean any wound with a warm solution of salted water on a piece of cotton wool promptly to prevent an abscess from occurring. If the wound is deep, seek immediate veterinary assistance.

Always consult a vet if you are in any doubt about what is wrong with your rabbit.

Heat Stroke

Rabbits are very vulnerable to heat stroke so be careful to protect your pet by ensuring that its run is not left in full sun, that it has a continuous supply of water and that the hutch is properly ventilated. A rabbit that does succumb to heatstroke should be wrapped in a thick towel that has been soaked in cold water and wrung out. If symptoms continue, seek immediate veterinary attention.

tip

Keep a record log

Jot down in a special notebook anything unusual you notice about your rabbit's appearance or behaviour and any medication you administer. This will be useful if you need to take your pet to see the vet.

DIAGNOSING AND TREATING HEALTH PROBLEMS

Symptoms	Likely causes	Treatment
Diarrhoea, weight loss, distended stomach	Too little hay (fibre) in the diet. Sudden change of diet. Coccidiosis, caused by a parasite, is a common cause of death in rabbits, especially youngsters. Keeping the hutch clean will help prevent it.	Seek immediate veterinary assistance.
Scratching, visible parasites on the rabbit's fur, discharge from ear	External parasites, which are not all visible. Fleas and mites are usually brought in via infested hay or from another infested animal. Mites can infect the ear canal of rabbits.	Seek veterinary assistance. A rabbit can be sprayed with an insecticidal spray or treated orally or by injection with anti-parasite cures. Never bathe your rabbit.
Bloated abdomen	Blocked gut, which may be caused by a sudden change in diet. Too little hay in the diet. Fur balls blocking the stomach.	Ensure that your rabbit is toileting normally and increase the amount of hay in the diet while reducing treats. Seek veterinary assistance if there is no improvement.
A soft or hard swelling on the rabbit's body	An abscess. This is usually the result of a bite that has become infected.	Seek veterinary assistance to lance the abscess. It will need cleansing thoroughly and in severe cases antibiotics may be needed.
Lots of white dandruff on the rabbit's neck and back, fur loss	A fungus called ringworm. This is a very infectious condition and can be transferred to and from other animals, including humans.	Difficult to eradicate. Seek veterinary advice for a suitable medication.
Swollen and sore genitalia. There may also be blisters on the mouth and around the nose.	Vent disease (also known as hutch burn), commonly caused by dirty hutches and may be transferred by mating. It is more common in does than in bucks.	Sores will need treatment with ointment obtained from your vet. Antibiotics will need to be administered in severe cases.

Sore hocks – redness on the base of the back feet	Pressure sores on the legs. Very common in rabbits with thin fur, such as Rexes, with very long claws or that are overweight.	Supply plenty of fresh bedding. Clipping nails and reducing the rabbit's weight may help. If there is no improvement, seek veterinary advice.
Lethargy, lack of droppings, extended belly	Constipation, which may be caused by a lack of water, a lack of fibre in the diet or a blockage.	Seek immediate veterinary assistance: death will occur if this condition is not treated immediately.
Very loose or liquid droppings, wet and dirty tail area	Diarrhoea. This may have a number of causes, including stress, change of diet and overfeeding with green food. It may also indicate coccidiosis (see left).	Avoid feeding green food and increase the hay in the diet. Make sure water is freely available. If the problem continues, seek veterinary advice immediately.
Sneezing, runny nose and eyes, generally poor condition	Could indicate a very contagious bacterial infection known as 'Snuffles'. Other causes may be a foreign body in the nose, or teeth or eye problems.	Seek veterinary advice. Vet will prescribe antibiotics for 'Snuffles' and can check teeth for over-growth and eyes for blockages.
Head tilted to one side	Suggests Pasteurella infection. Also possibility of stroke or neurological problem.	Seek veterinary advice immediately.
Rabbit not eating, dribbling, runny eyes	Most likely cause is teeth problems, possibly as the result of poor diet or old age.	Seek veterinary assistance. Ensure there is plenty of fibre in the diet to naturally wear the teeth down.
Swollen eyelids, swellings at the base of the ears, around the nose and genitalia	Myxomatosis, a viral disease, which is transferred by biting insects and is always fatal.	There is no cure, but a vaccination is available from vets in areas with a high incidence of the disease.
Sudden death, occasionally blood around nose	Rabbit Viral Haemorrhagic Disease (VHD), a very infectious disease passed by contact. Few visible symptoms.	VHD is always fatal, but vaccinations against the disease are available from your vet.

Developing Your Hobby

Learning more, exhibiting rabbits and breeding advice

Once you have had your rabbit for a while, you may want to further your knowledge about your pet or even to expand your new hobby into new areas. For example, you may want to think about keeping a different breed, keeping a house rabbit, going to a show or even breeding rabbits.

While there are other good books and websites that you can research – there is a list of recommended ones on page 64 – nothing beats getting together with others who share your enthusiasm. Contact one of the national societies (see page 64) for details of others in your area.

At a rabbit show, each registered entrant will be allocated its own show pen.

howing rabbits

The procedures adopted at rabbit shows vary from country to country, but you can find out details of shows and showing from your country's governing body (see page 64). If you want to exhibit your rabbit, it must be pure bred and can be entered in one of several classes depending on breed, colour and age.

In the UK, rabbit shows are governed by the British Rabbit Council (BRC) and are star-rated, from small, local 1-star shows to prestigious 5-star ones. Rabbit shows in the USA are not graded. There will usually be at least two judges at even the smallest show and their role will be to assess each rabbit by how closely in conforms to the Breed Standard. Each Breed Standard states exactly what each breed of rabbit should look like – its size, build, head shape, colour, coat length etc. A judge will then compare the rabbits entered against each other in the same class.

Pet shows

If your pet rabbit is a crossbreed – many sold in pet shops are – you can still enter it into a pet show. Here the judge will be looking primarily at the overall health, condition and cleanliness of the rabbit and awards are given on the basis of how well you have cared for your pet rather than on whether it conforms to a Breed Standard.

Even if your rabbit does not conform to a Breed Standard, it may still win an award at a pet show provided that you have cared for it well.

REGISTRATION RINGS

In the UK, breeders put a ring around one of the hindlegs of a pure-bred rabbit that shows the rabbit's year of birth and registration number. The ring is fitted when the rabbit is three to nine weeks old and a rabbit will not be eligible to be shown without such a ring.

If your rabbit arrives with such a ring you will need to check this regularly throughout your pet's life. It should be loose enough to turn easily around the leg.

In the USA and many other countries, rabbits are tattooed with a number inside one ear instead of being rung. American pure-bred rabbits are also issued with a pedigree.

Breeding Rabbits

Before you think about breeding rabbits you need to ask yourself why you want to breed this litter and what you will do with the babies. You also need to make sure that you breed only from healthy, well-handled animals. There are already far more baby rabbits being bred than there are good homes for them so make sure that you are not simply adding to the number of unwanted pets.

Good breeding practice

Always take the doe to the buck's cage for mating, never the other way round, and return her to her cage immediately after mating has taken place.

Handle the doe as little as possible while she is pregnant, especially during the later days. She will need more food while pregnant, but increase her rations gradually until they are about double th normal amount.

About 25 days after mating has occurred, you will need to provide the doe with a nest box and extra bedding. When she is ready to give birth – about 30 days after mating – she will pluck he fur to line this nest.

Avoid disturbing the nest as much as possible once the doe has given birth to her litter. These kittens are about three weeks old.

The growing litter

Newborn kittens are blind, naked and helpless. They will open their eyes at about 10 days old, by which time they will have grown some fur. Soon afterwards, they will leave the nest and begin to explore. It is now time to increase the food supply again as they will begin to nibble at solid food, although they will not be fully weaned until they are about six to eight weeks old. At this stage, remove the mother from the cage and, after a few more days, divide the babies into single-sex groups. They are now ready to go to their new homes.

This 10-day old baby rabbit has just opened its eyes and will soon be exploring its environment.

t six weeks old, ese young Lops re weaned and nearly ready to go to their new homes.

fter the birth

The number of babies (kittens) in the litter will depend on the breed; in general, larger breeds have larger litters. A first-time mother will often have a smaller litter than usual and may lose her babies through inexperience.

After the birth, check for any dead babies and remove them, but otherwise disturb the new mother and her young as little as possible. A nursing doe will be very territorial and may become agitated to the point of killing her babies if you intrude on her nest. Increase her food rations to about three times the normal amount while she is suckling and make sure she has plenty of fresh water available.

FALSE PREGNANCY

Sometimes a doe, mated or not, will appear to be pregnant and will even begin to prepare a nest – running around or digging with a mouth full of hay or fur – but no babies will appear. This is called a 'false pregnancy' and can be a common occurrence with does that are never used for breeding. Such does will generally be happier if they are spayed.

Further Information

RECOMMENDED BOOKS

A Petlove Guide to Rabbits and Guinea Pigs Alderton, David (Interpet Publishing, 1986)
Training Your Pet Rabbit Bartlett, Patricia (Barron's, 2002)
Rabbitlopaedia, A Complete Guide to Rabbit Care Brown, Meg, and Richardson, Virginia (Ringpress Books, 2000)
Living With a Houserabbit Dykes, Linda, and Flack, Helen (Interpet Publishing, 2003)
The Rabbit Handbook Gendron, Karen (Barron's, 2000)
The House Rabbit Handbook Harriman, Marinell (Drollery Press, 1995)
Care For Your Rabbit Hearne, Tina (RSPCA Guide, Collins, 1990)
Pet Owner's Guide to the Dwarf Rabbit Leewood, Hazel (Ringpress Books, 1999)
Why Does My Rabbit...? McBride, Anne (Souvenir Press, 2000)
How to Have a Relaxed Rabbit Magnus, Emma (Pet Behaviour Centre, 2001)
Pet Owner's Guide to the Rabbit Mays, Marianne (Ringpress Books, 1995)
Gold Medal Guide: Golden Tips for Keeping Your First Rabbit O'Neill, Amanda (Interpet Publishing, 2004)
Getting To Know Your Rabbit Page, Gill (Interpet Publishing, 2000)
The Essential Rabbit Siino, Betsy Sikora (Howell Book House, 1998)
Rabbits – A Complete Pet Owner's Manual Wegler, Monica (Barron's, 1999)

CLUBS

British Rabbit Council, Purefoy House, 7 Kirkgate, Newark, Nottinghamshire, NG24 1AD, UK. Tel: +44(0)1636 676042.
American Rabbit Breeders' Association, P.O. Box 426, Bloomington, IL 61702, USA.

RECOMMENDED WEBSITES

http://www.allaboutpets.org.uk/spintro.html
http://www.furandfeather.co.uk
http://www.rabbitbehaviour.co.uk
http://rabbitrehome.org.uk
http://www.rabbitwelfarefund.co.uk
http://thebrc.org

PICTURE CREDITS

The majority of the pictures in this book were taken by Neil Sutherland and are the copyright of Interpet Publishing. Other pictures are also the copyright of Interpet Publishing, with the exception of the following: page 14(R): Sally Anne Thompson/Animal Photography; pages 15(T), 18(C), 23(BL): *Fur and Feather* magazine; page 32: Angela Hampton/RSPCAphotolibrary.